Pack Your Parachute

Keeping Peril Out of Your Estate Plan!

Francisco P. Sirvent

Learn from others how Francisco Sirvent and Keystone Law Firm has helped them gain peace of mind with their guaranteed estate plan:

Keystone Law Firm, has taken great care of me from the start! Francisco goes above and beyond the scope of his job to make sure you know he is there for you. I wish every Law firm had the same integrity and ethics that Francisco has. I know if they did, there would be a great deal less work for the judges to have to deal with. I consider Francisco a friend that cares about my best interests!

Ken B.

I want to thank the Francisco Sirvent for helping me solve my problems. Francisco is the "real deal." I read his biography and if anything he is too humble regarding his ability to focus on and tackle the issues head on. In addition, his is style is unmatched; incredible listener. I will contact his law group for any legal issue, first before I do anything. I trust him and his judgment that much. There is something very special here. He is simply the best.

John H.

After working with 4 other attorneys (all of whom "fit the profile" of your typical lawyer), Francisco actually sat down and listened to me. It was great having a lawyer who treated me like a friend, not just another client.

Jeff. H.

Francisco Sirvent consulted with us previously and again after a major change in our family situation. He exhibits the utmost professionalism combined with an extremely personable attitude and the ability to explain legal terms in laymen's language. He shows a genuine interest in the entire family involved in the legal decisions, including the request for family pictures of those not involved in the meetings. At no point did we feel rushed. Francisco truly provides the time and explanations required to make needed decisions. We have already recommended Francisco to others for the legal services he provides. One of the many things we appreciated was the inclusion of the personal statement of faith in the material we received. The experience to date with Francisco has been 180 from any previous legal experience. We will continue to be in touch with the office of course. As just one example of the thoughtfulness of Francisco, he sent a very practical and interesting diagram by email after our meeting. We have complete trust in Francisco's ability to apply the law to our particular situation and to truly care about our family's long term welfare. He made us very comfortable with the process of doing our trust.

M.B. and J.B.

Copyright © 2018 by Francisco P. Sirvent

All rights reserved. No part of this book may be used or reproduced in any manner whatsoever without prior written consent of the author, except as provided by the United States of America copyright law.

Published by Keystone Law Firm, Chandler, AZ

ISBN 9781709580314

Additional copies are available at special quantity discounts for bulk purchases for sales promotions, premiums, fundraising, and educational use.

For more information, please contact: Francisco P. Sirvent, **(480) 418-1776**

Contact the author directly at Info@keystonelawfirm.com

The Publisher and Author make no representations or warranties with respect to the accuracy or completeness of the contents of this work and specifically disclaim all warranties, including without limitation warranties of fitness for a particular purpose. No warranty may be created or extended by sales or promotional materials. The advice and strategies contained herein may not be suitable for every situation. This work is sold with the understanding that the publisher is not engaged in rendering legal, account or other professional services. If professional assistance is required, the services of a competent professional person should be sought. Neither the Publisher nor the Author shall be liable for damages arising here from. The fact that an organization or website is referred to in this work as a citation and/or potential source of further information does not mean the Author or Publisher endorses the information the organization or website may provide or recommendations it may make. Further, readers should be aware that the Internet websites listed in this work may have changed or disappeared between when this work was written and when it was read.

Printed in the United States of America.

Learn MORE about how
WE can help
YOU get your affairs in order

480-418-1776

Call our office TODAY!

Make your appointment for your Discovery Hour

There's no substitute for being prepared!

We'll create your guaranteed estate plan!

Table of Contents

Learn MORE about how WE can create an IRON-CLAD estate plan for you	5
Acknowledgements	9
Foreword	10
Introduction	13
A much better way to help people	16
Peril #1	18
Peril #2	20
Peril #3	22
Peril #4	24
Peril #5	27
Peril #6	31
Peril #7	35
Peril #8	37
Peril #9	39
Peril #10	41
Peril #11	43
Peril #12	45
Learn MORE about how WE can create an IRON-CLAD estate plan for you	61
My last words: Francisco P. Sirvent	62

To Bella, Gabe, Sophie, and Zach:

You won't have a mess to clean up.

Acknowledgements

So many people have tolerated me during the process of writing this book. I can't possibly name you all here, but a few have seen what it looks like for an attorney to undertake this type of effort. This project would not be in the readers' hands were it not for my especially patient wife, Nicole, and Sheryl at the office. Thank you, thank you, thank you! ...for walking along side me, encouraging me, and correcting me each time it was needed.

And to the many colleagues who have said "You can do it" and "You should do it"; thank you for challenging me and setting the expectations high. Hopefully this brings answers to many people who need them.

Foreword

By Francisco P. Sirvent
Attorney and Problem Solver at Law™

Probates are a government-sanctioned invasion of privacy. Every client who has experienced it firsthand would have done anything to avoid it.

As an estate planning attorney and owner of Keystone Law Firm, I have seen plenty of people dragged through conservatorships and guardianships—expensive and complicated probate lawsuits.

People get dragged through these cases only because they never took the time to arrange their legal affairs.

The problem is so extreme and widespread that the court must use court-appointed attorneys to take the cases on—like public defenders. Every year, millions and millions of Arizonans' hard-earned dollars go to these attorneys instead of paying for their grandchildren's education or a son or daughter's down payment on their first house.

Probate is a voluntary "tax" because all you have to do to avoid it is make your decisions and get your estate matters squared away with a qualified estate-planning attorney.

Each and every day, I am driven to help people put plans in place that will allow them to keep their dollars and property from falling into the hands of probate attorneys.

One particular client was forced to become the court-appointed guardian and conservator over her husband, who suffers from early onset dementia. After their first thirty years of marriage, they received the bad news that the husband could no longer manage his own financial affairs. It wasn't long before she learned she would need to hire me, along with another attorney appointed by the court to represent her husband, to drag their lives into the court. Before long, this "simple" matter involved her, the judge, me, the court-appointed attorney—plus a third and even a FOURTH attorney—all to win her the right to manage the family's investments, pay their bills, and ultimately take care of her dependent spouse. The matter involved a very trying, emotionally exhausting, and incredibly expensive first couple of years.

Today, my client suffers through the pain of watching her husband slip deeper and deeper into dementia as she continues to care for his full-time needs. If that isn't difficult enough, she is required to report everything she does to the court while being challenged by court-appointed attorneys about the decisions she makes and the actions she takes. On occasion, the judge attacks her for not doing things the way the judge would have liked, and here's the ringer—she is responsible for paying all of these people—one fighting FOR her and many fighting AGAINST her.

As her attorney, it has been incredibly frustrating and deeply discouraging. The guardianship and conservatorship probate courts were ostensibly created to protect people who could not protect themselves. But how do people protect themselves from the "protectors" when the protectors, that is the probate courts, are creating the majority of the problems for incapacitated people?

That's what Arizona's probate system does. That's how it works.

The probate matters that occur **during your life** are the absolute worst type of court cases. When it's simple to **OPT OUT** of that nightmare system, why wouldn't everyone?

And I love, truly love being able to do the things we can to help people avoid that problem forever. It has become my life's work to educate as many people as possible about the 12 Perils of Estate Planning and how to avoid them.

Introduction

In 2009, our local newspaper, The Arizona Republic, printed an article about the local probate courts. One of the investigative reporters started looking into the Arizona probate system and eventually found the kind of story that makes every journalist salivate. A huge investigative report resulted, and the matter wound up gaining the attention of the Arizona Supreme Court. The Arizona Supreme Court began to realize there was a systemic problem—one they knew existed, but now realized was far worse than ever imagined.

The precipitating article was about a gentleman named Mr. Sleeth. His story is one of the most egregious and atrocious stories of financial abuse most people will ever hear. The truth is Mr. Sleeth's story kicked off a firestorm that ultimately led to significant changes in our probate court system, our trust code, and many other Arizona laws. Keep in mind: everything that happened to him was perfectly legal, and was even approved by the probate court system.

Mr. Sleeth's case involved a guardianship case—a type of probate case that happens while the person is still alive. For several painful, expensive years, Mr. Sleeth was dragged through the courts and lost about a half million dollars.

Finally, someone came alongside Mr. Sleeth—someone who helped him, fought for him, and was able to recover close to $200,000 of those fees.

It was a long nightmare to endure.

I share Mr. Sleeth's story as one more reason why I started an estate-planning firm, and why my priority is to help as many people as I can avoid the expense and heartache that occurs when they are not prepared. Many people do not really understand that estate planning is not just about what happens after we die. Naturally, we want to be prepared for when that happens, yet there are many very important things that happen while we are still alive that can rattle anyone if he or she is not prepared.

I have written this book to help you avoid the 12 most common mistakes people make in preparing an estate plan. I hope as you read, you will learn all of the different elements that comprise a full estate plan. I will explain all of the details about wills, trusts and Arizona's probate system and how each of them work.

Estate planning is what I do, and my number one goal is to help you protect what you have.

Many people put off getting their estate planning done until it's too late. My firm, Keystone Law Firm, also helps people who are being dragged through the probate system. While I cannot turn back the clock and put their plans in place, I can offer reassurance and compassion to their family when it is time for their estate to move through that terrible system.

Today, our firm is helping people just like you protect over $440,000,000 from the probate system; that's the total net worth of our clients' assets we are responsible to protect. This makes me incredibly proud and humbled. Because of my help, my clients' plans are consistently updated, they are correctly maintained, all are error-free, and each is guaranteed NO PROBATE.

After more than 10 years, I still enjoy coming to work every day. And that's why I decided to write this small book. I wanted more people to have the facts so that they can educate themselves BEFORE they even visit my firm.

A much better way to help people

At the beginning of my law career, I worked as a trial lawyer. I learned very quickly about the typical way lawyers earn money. Most attorneys charge in six-minute increments, and bill clients accordingly. Each and every time you pick up the phone to speak to your attorney—even just to ask a simple question and receive a terse confirmation—that little phone exchange is a six-minute increment. In less than thirty days, you can find a bill in your mailbox for that six-minute increment.

When I discovered this truth as a young attorney, I found it disturbing. Every day, I worked on clients' cases solving their problems. Then, on the first of the month, a new problem would arrive: their bill.

This frustration created a desire in me to look for a new way to practice law. What I really wanted was to find a way I could continue to help solve people's problems, but without creating new problems. I wanted to discover a way to complete projects for a flat, fixed cost. This way, I could share exactly what I would be doing to help them up front and offer them a firm, fixed price tag. I wanted to be a "Problem Solver at Law™" where there is no surprise bill at the end.

And that's how I landed on estate planning as a way of using my law degree, my experience, and my desire to help.

As you read this and learn about the many aspects of estate planning, you will likely think of questions. At the end of each chapter, I have given you a page for notes. As you read, keep a pen handy and jot down your questions or ideas on those pages. When you want to get your questions answered, you will have them handy when we meet. As you read, consider what it is you are hoping to achieve with your estate plan.

At the end of each chapter, I have included a brief scoring system to help you to better understand YOUR estate plan situation. Take a moment after you read each chapter to score yourself.

How confident are you that you have Peril # solved?

Circle One Number:

(Not solved) 1 2 3 4 5 6 7 8 9 10 (Perfectly solved!)

Peril #1

Failure to maintain control of your healthcare decisions is the first Peril. The reason this one is so important to avoid is because here in the US, eighty-five percent of all deaths will occur in a clinical setting; most people do not die at home. Instead, people pass away in assisted living facilities, nursing homes, or the hospital. Preparing your healthcare directives is not only a gift for you and your best treatment; it is also a gift to your family. When you become incapacitated and are in one of these facilities surrounded by your licensed clinicians, they request the correct legal documents so that they may give you properly authorized care. Without these documents, the entire scenario becomes complicated.

If the facility learns that the proper legal instructions do not exist, the facility can demand a court-appointed guardian. This is the last resort for anyone who has not done planning ahead of time. The guardianship process works like this: somebody—your significant other, your child or your close relative—approaches the court with a request. They might say, "Judge, my wife is in a coma. We have no legal documents in place and I need to make some health care decisions for her. I am requesting the authority to do that."

Only a judge can approve this action, and obtaining this authority will be time consuming, expensive, public, and challenging.

When you take the time to put your health care decisions in the proper legal format, you have given your family a gift. This is critically important at the moment a doctor tells you or your loved ones that you are no longer able to make reasonable decisions for yourself. The sad truth is this can happen to any of us, at any moment. If and when your provider says the words, "I am afraid this person can no longer make his or her own decisions," it is already too late to put any legal protections in place. When you do formalize these decisions, there are no unknowns. The professionals know exactly what you want and can follow them through immediately. Your family—who are already distraught over your health and physical condition—can focus on their love for you and getting you the best care rather than dealing with the stress of hiring lawyers and preparing to speak with a judge.

How confident are you that you have Peril #1 solved?

Circle One Number:

(Not solved) 1 2 3 4 5 6 7 8 9 10 (Perfectly solved!)

Peril #2

The Health Insurance Portability and Accountability Act, or HIPAA as it is commonly known, is a 1996 law that was established to give Americans control over personal health care decisions and records. Sin #2 is failing to prepare for HIPAA. This federal law locks down all of your medical information as confidential. Your medical records are meant only for your eyes and for those of your healthcare providers. None of your medical information is open for discussion or disclosure with anyone else without your written permission. While it is simple to prepare, the truth is many Americans do not have this document formally drafted and signed. The absence of this document can make an already emotional and possibly life-threatening situation all the more difficult.

Here's the problem. The moment we are unable to communicate with our healthcare providers, because we are incapacitated or are in surgery, we are no longer capable of granting permission to anyone. This means that your healthcare information is locked down. In order to gain access to it, the least desirable option is to have a guardian appointed by the court. If you are seeking to access your loved one's information, you would then go to court and inform the judge: "Your Honor, we didn't do anything to prepare for this, and we now need access to know what room our loved one is in at the hospital."

Only a judge can grant such a request and appoint a guardian.

HIPAA was established to protect our medical privacy. In order to avoid the unintended consequences of this law, you must take action to prepare.

How confident are you that you have Peril #2 solved?

Circle One Number:

(Not solved) 1 2 3 4 5 6 7 8 9 10 (Perfectly solved!)

Peril #3

Medical retirement planning helps people prepare for the last three to five years of life—easily the most expensive period of living. While I include this in my checklist, this is more of a financial planning matter. The families of those living in nursing homes or other health care facilities often are surprised by the overwhelming expenses facing their loved one.

As an estate-planning attorney, I prepare the legal plan for my clients and help them consider all possible scenarios that could arise as they age. That's why #3 remains on my list. While you still have time to plan, you need to answer this question: "How will you pay for your care when you are at the end of your life?" The reality is that long-term care is sickeningly expensive. In Maricopa County, the average cost is $6,000 a month. When you add this up, you or your estate could be charged more than $70,000 per year. For those without a sizeable nest egg, expenses such as these can be catastrophic.

The reality is there are only three options to pay for long term care:

1. Will you self-fund this expense?
2. Will you structure your estate plan and trust in a way to qualify for public benefits?
3. Will you transfer the risk to an insurance company?

If you don't plan for this, the risks are that you'll eventually go broke, your spouse will end up penniless, or you won't have anything to leave your children.

There are many variations of long-term care policies, a metaphorical sea of options. While many of the older historical policies have gone by the wayside, there are some new ones that make sense. The bottom line is you will need to learn and identify the option that works best for you and choose one while you still have time.

How confident are you that you have Peril #3 solved?

Circle One Number:

(Not solved) 1 2 3 4 5 6 7 8 9 10 (Perfectly solved!)

Peril #4

Peril #4 is failing to protect your finances if you should become incapacitated. Many believe estate planning only deals with issues after you die. We are already a third of the way through the 12 Perils of Estate Planning and we haven't even touched on problems that arise after death; we are talking about issues that are important to those still living. With typical estate planning, most of the discussion centers on what happens after we die. However, a comprehensive estate plan provides legal protections while we are still alive.

In many cases, the moment you become incapacitated is the moment your finances will be locked down 100 percent and frozen by your banks or investment companies. Becoming incapacitated has many different meanings and it is not limited to the most extreme example: you are in a coma. You could be laid up on your back and unable to move from an injury. You could have slight memory loss or any stage of dementia or Alzheimer's disease. If any of these things happen and you do not have all the legal protections in places, you are at risk for needing to establish a conservatorship.

A conservatorship is the probate court's process of appointing someone to pay your bills, direct your investments, take distributions from your IRA account, sell your house, or conduct your personal financial business with legal authority.

The problem with conservatorships (and guardianships)—both probate cases that happen when we're alive—is that they are incredibly expensive and public, meaning everything is discussed and decided in a public courtroom between you, a judge, and a court-appointed attorney. Sometimes there is even a third attorney called a guardian *ad litem*.

Remember the client I described at the beginning of the book, the one who is taking care of her husband? Despite the fact that they had a trust and power of attorney, she is being forced to work through the probate courts in a conservatorship and will continue to do so for the rest of her husband's life because their plan was not done correctly, was not up to date, and their attorney did not help implement their plan.

In this scenario, I represent her. Her husband has his own attorney, just like in a divorce. The entire experience FEELS like a divorce. Compounding the matter is the attorney who was appointed to act as the guardian ad litem. Guardian ad litem are appointed by the court to represent the "best interests" of the person who is incapacitated.

That particular client's case began five years and over $40,000 in attorney's fees ago. The whole fiasco took us about a year to secure full legal authority to do everything she needed.

A guardian *ad litem* was appointed in this case to assure the husband's "best interest" was thoroughly protected and that no one was taking advantage of him; which, in my opinion, was an exercise in futility. Despite there being NO evidence that she would do anything inappropriate with her authority, these protections can be required by the court when someone's estate planning is not 100% perfect.

Saving clients from lifetime probate nightmares is my passion.

After experiencing cases in which things were not done 100% perfectly, I became motivated to educate as many people as possible about probate nightmares. I can help those nightmares be avoided.

You now begin to understand that while having parts of an estate plan in place may be somewhat useful, having one or more parts outdated or incomplete can have a profoundly negative effect on our lives and the lives of our loved ones.

How confident are you that you have Peril #4 solved?

Circle One Number:

(Not solved) 1 2 3 4 5 6 7 8 9 10 (Perfectly solved!)

Peril #5
Guest Author, John Hagensen, Keystone Wealth Partners, LLC

Peril #5 is more about doing the wrong thing, rather than doing nothing at all. The fifth Peril causes you to lose 20%-30% (or more) of your nest egg due to making emotional decisions with your investments. John Hagensen, the owner of our sister company, Keystone Wealth Partners, will provide us with the information for this Peril.

You might be thinking, "This book is about Estate Planning. What does a financial advisor have to add?"

Your estate plan is only as good as whatever it actually is protecting. Imagine having a $10,000 safe at home that holds 100% of your life savings. Now imagine that savings consists entirely of Enron stock certificates. How valuable is that safe now? An estate plan is the same way. If you have an iron-clad estate plan that is meant to protect all of your assets, but your assets are poorly managed or not managed at all, what good was that estate plan?

Are you a human being? Of course! Here's the great part about human: we empathize, we're relational, and we have emotions. Here's the bad part about being human: those emotions hardwire us to make terrible investment decisions. During the last twenty-five years, have you ever felt emotional about your investments? Allow me to jog your memory—perhaps you did in 2001 or 2008? If you are like many others, you didn't have peace of mind about what was happening during those times, and that insecurity caused you to move money around in ways that—in hindsight—were pretty foolish.

I've found in working with hundreds of investors that our emotions, especially our emotions tied to our financial well-being, can spark quick decisions that have long-term impact. These quick, emotional decisions are the most dangerous things anyone can do when it comes to their retirement dollars. I am talking about decisions based on fear, speculation, greed, loyalty, and envy. If I could share just one piece of information with every investor, it would be the results of a DALBAR study.

DALBAR, the nation's leading financial services market research firm, monitors investor behavior. They are an industry standard regarding investor behavior. To help demonstrate some perspective, let's go back to 1984 and look at one scenario. If you were an investor in 1984, it's possible you were unsure about what mutual funds to buy, which broker to trust, or whether you should be invested in the market. If instead of trying to figure it all out, you said to yourself, "I don't know what to do. I'm just going to put all my money in the S&P 500—the 500 largest US stocks—and I'm never going to move it. I'm just going to leave it there until I retire."

Here's what would have happened with your investment throughout the last 30 years. Your money would have earned a whopping 11.1% per year on average for the last 30 years. Can you believe that? Your friends would think you were an investment genius: "Wow! How did you do that? Did you buy at the bottom and sell at the top; did you get out of the S&P 500 at the start of '08 and then get back in right at the bottom? How did you time that so well? Who is your broker? Can I get their card? They must be a guru."

The truth is this: to obtain those results, you did nothing more than work hard, spend time with your family, and avoid doing anything emotional with your money. These results allow you to enjoy 25 times your initial investment—all because you employed the simplest strategy possible, and then controlled your behavior.

The real problem with this: during the same 30 year period in the U.S., the average stock investor earned less than 4% per year. Ouch! Imagine all the dreams, goals, and plans that have been lost because of the 7% shortfall—you might call this a tax on emotions.

I meet with investors all day long to share this information and it's common for me to receive a lukewarm response to "the market". Many people possess a general sentiment that they do not want to "play the market". It's a natural mindset for someone who has been earning 3-4 percent a year for the last 30 years. Who gets excited about that? Nobody. On the other hand, if everybody you played tennis with, golfed with, and barbecued with had been making 11-12 percent for the last 30 years, their opinion of the market would be vastly different.

"It's the greatest wealth-creation tool in the history of the world! Wow, we have 25 times our money."

Unfortunately, the data shows very few people have actually achieved that because of the emotional decisions we make with our money. Combine that with the fact that many of us work with a financial advisor that is compensated based upon the movement of our money. It's true. When an advisor is paid based on the number of times our money is transferred and moved (the number of buys and sells), a very shaky foundation for seeking investment success over longer periods of time is created.

Here's another way to think about this. Most Americans intellectually know how to be physically fit. It's pretty simple, right? East less, move more. Most of us WANT to be more fit, so why is it we are not all walking around with six-packs?

It's because we do not DO what we KNOW how to do.

Investing is very, very similar. The rules of how to be successful in retirement and to protect and grow your money are simple, but they are not easy. Data proves this over and over. In the last 20 years, if you had started with a $10,000 investment but were out of the market for the best rolling ten-day period, the potential of $54,000 shrinks all of the way down to $27,000. In missing these 10 days, you would have lost half of your returns over that 20-year period for being out for only ten days. Granted, it is highly unlikely that you would have left the market for those specific ten days that just happened to be the best ten days. But I share this to illustrate how speculative it is to try to think that you're going to know when to be invested and when not to be invested in the market. It is impossible to know consistently when to "get in" and "get out" over the long term.

How confident are you that you have Peril #5 solved?

Circle One Number:

(Not solved) 1 2 3 4 5 6 7 8 9 10 (Perfectly solved!)

Peril #6

Guest Author, John Hagensen, Keystone Wealth Partners, LLC

To explain Peril #6, we must agree on one thing: financial advisors are NOT non-profit businesses. We are professionals with expertise and we earn money. But how? Peril #6 is losing returns due to hidden fees and commissions.

Many financial advisors earn their living through fees, commissions, and other expenses. But if they are too high, they can significantly erode your investment earnings totals.

Imagine you have a medical need and you go to a doctor who prescribes some medication and a specific therapy regimen. If your doctor was paid like most financial advisors, how much would you trust that doctor's prescription?

If doctors were paid like financial advisors, they would get paid by pharmaceutical companies based on the number of prescriptions they write. Do you think that might create a conflict of interest? If that doctor is paid a $20,000 commission for recommending one medicine but only $2,000 for recommending another, which medicine do you think is going to be recommended more often? Worse, imagine if all you really needed was an Advil, a glass of orange juice, and some rest—for which the doctor is paid $0?

It's clear to see that even the most moral and ethical physician would be tempted to justify prescribing the medicine that pays the highest commission (maybe even just occasionally). This is why the FDA does not allow pharmaceutical reps to spoil physicians any longer.

Unfortunately, the financial industry has operated this way for 50 years. It is no wonder so many investors have only earned 3.5% a year while the market is making 11%. The average investor cannot figure it out. Yet his or her advisors are enjoying two homes, fancy cars, and luxurious offices. The reason? Typical advisors are paid commissions, which vary from stock to stock, and mutual fund to mutual fund. It creates conflicts of interests with their "advice". Plus, there are many other hidden charges.

A telltale sign that your advisor does not work for you is shown on their business card. What I mean by this is when you get the business card of an advisor, the card clearly says:

Mr. Financial Advisor,

Registered Representative of Merrill Lynch, UBS or Morgan Stanley.

These advisors do not work for you; they are working for their company. While this is a typical way of doing business, it is vastly different from the way we work with our investment clients at Keystone. I encourage anyone to work with a <u>registered investment advisory</u> firm that is not paid commissions. I am paid a fee *by my clients* to work for them. I earn the same fee regardless of the investment choices my clients make.

When you are selecting an advisor to work with you and your life's earnings, it's critical that you set yourself up for success. When you choose an advisor who is compensated based on how often your money is moved, or which investment they advise, you are choosing to put their financial interests ahead of your own.

What are some of these hidden costs? Take variable annuities, for example. All of the desirable results are fully disclosed when the product is sold, yet the internal expenses range from 3.5-4% a year. These costs are never shared with you. It's very common for a half million dollar variable annuity to charge you upwards of $29,000 each year for "internal expenses". I share this information every day with people who do not understand these insurance products. It's a built-in cost that never appears on any statement or online account. When you discover this information and begin doing the math, it can be shocking to consider the erosion on your earnings over 10 or 20 years. It's unbelievable.

Allow me to illustrate something very interesting. Let's imagine you saved one half percent each year on these fees by working with an objective advisor who is knowledgeable in helping you to analyze your investments and make objective recommendations. Let's keep everything else equal for this illustration. In ten years, that half percent would earn $42,000 more in ten years, and $120,000 over the next 20 years.

It's astounding, isn't it? Think about this from an estate planning perspective. The people that you love, your kids, or your charities, would have another $120,000! Do you think that could help your children or your grandkids more than it would help the insurance companies? Of course it could.

Know your fees and costs:
- What is your all-in annual cost on your portfolio?
- What are you paying your advisor annually?
- What are you paying the fund companies?
- What are you paying in commissions?
- Is a third party paying your advisor?
- What are your insurance contracts charging you?
- How are these fees paid?

How confident are you that you have Peril #6 solved?

Circle One Number:

(Not solved) 1 2 3 4 5 6 7 8 9 10 (Perfectly solved!)

Peril #7

You may have noticed that many of the Perils each have dollar signs attached and Peril #7 is no different: failing to plan for and understand estate taxes—a costly mistake.

Estate tax is a tax that all Americans face, similar to income taxes paid annually, but estate taxes are levied just once, upon our death. Each of us is offered a certain amount of assets that are exempt from the estate tax, called the "exemption." According to federal law, those who die in 2018 can pass property equal to their exemption, $11.18 million dollars, and pay zero estate tax. That figure includes the sum total of everything: real estate value, business value, life insurance benefits, bank accounts, personal property—everything you own or have an interest in.

Today, married couples each get a $11.18 million exemption—combined for a total of more than $22 million. Therefore the estate tax affects very few people. Before this change emerged in 2013, the exemption amount changed every year. This created a never-ending problem because Congress was forced to act every year before the exemption amount decreased to pre-2001 levels. In each instance, it caused a constant risk that the exemption could revert back to $1 million per couple (rather than per individual). If this happened, it would present a problem for far more people because, when life insurance death benefits included a million dollar term policy, the tax would be a whopping 55%!

Federal tax laws are in a constant state of flux. Each year there are proposals to change them, to reduce the exemption, to increase the exemption—all because it is a political bargaining chip in Washington D.C. My job as an estate planning attorney is to watch the laws, watch my clients' net worth, and monitor the ceilings so that if their individual net worth grows too close to the limits, or the limits drop, I can recommend some additional protective measures. It's not hard to avoid the estate tax when you know all of the tools available. I work to make sure you don't end up sending 40 percent of your excess assets to the I.R.S.

How confident are you that you have Peril #7 solved?

Circle One Number:

(Not solved) 1 2 3 4 5 6 7 8 9 10 (Perfectly solved!)

Peril #8

Peril #8 is failing to protect adult children from themselves. The first thing most married people think about as they prepare their estate is taking care of one another. The second natural concern is thinking about their children or other beneficiaries. Many people are not aware that grown children might need inheritance protection. As I write this, I am pointing a finger directly at me. I am part of the generation of adult children who need inheritance protection.

About four or five years ago, I worked with a client to draft his estate plan. As we worked together, he was adamant that his children were financially solid and everyone got along great. His desire was that everyone would divide the money evenly when he passed, period. A short while later, my client passed away and the two children that he appointed came in and we started wrapping up all of his affairs. After a few months, the time came to prepare the distribution checks. There were five adult children, ranging in age from 50s to early 60s. Unfortunately, when that time came, two of those five people had filed bankruptcy. We had the estate ready to distribute five ways equally, but sadly, 40% of his estate (two of the five shares) went to the bankruptcy trustees instead of his two children.

I know he wouldn't have wanted that.

He could never have foreseen the 2008 financial crisis causing two of his kids to lose their jobs and be forced to file bankruptcy.

He could never have known that. It's a difficult yet realistic example where a different decision in the estate planning process could have made a huge difference. There are simple ways to guard an inheritance from bankruptcy. In 2010, Arizona passed the Arizona Trust Code. This new law allows us to protect inheritances from bankruptcy, creditors, lawsuits, and even a divorcing son- or daughter-in-law. Arizona is among the few states that allow you to protect your inheritance from seizure if your beneficiaries' spouse files for divorce. If your beneficiary gets into a car accident, their inheritance is safe. If they file bankruptcy, their inheritance is safe. A "protective trust" can be made part of your plan.

How confident are you that you have Peril #8 solved?

Circle One Number:

(Not solved) 1 2 3 4 5 6 7 8 9 10 (Perfectly solved!)

Peril #9

Peril #9 is failing to leave behind your values. Committing this sin would be a missed opportunity to share your values with your family. Traditionally, estate planning is all about a plan to distribute your money and property when you die. Yet, there is more to pass on than just your assets. There are your values.

Perhaps you have said, "I hope my last check to the morgue bounces. I hope I spend it all!" To that, I say "Great, call me the day before you pass away so we can get everything organized, ok?" If only we knew when that day would be.

I am not a traditional estate-planning attorney, and Keystone is not a traditional firm. We have established a special process for estate planning where we want to help you transition everything you value to its rightful place, the place you say it should go. This means helping you find the right place for your property, your money and, to us, it also means your values. We want to help you take what's important to you and make sure that we include it as part of your estate plan. As part of our process, we encourage you to communicate the values attached to those decisions and actions included in your plan. We want your beneficiaries to know what's important to you, what you stand for, and the things you have accomplished in your life.

In the last years of his life, my grandpa sat down and wrote different stories and thoughts about his whole life. Growing up on a farm in Nebraska. Getting in trouble with his buddies. Rebuilding cars. Going to the war. Marrying my grandmother.

He wrote all of these little vignettes and experiences on his old computer. He then compiled it and photocopied it at Kinko's and sent each of his kids and grandkids their own copy before he passed away. I will never forget when I received one of those collections of my grandfather's tales. I loved reading all of his crazy stories. I was struck by his incredible wisdom and all of the experiences he shared for me to learn from. When I read those 200 pages, I felt like I had grown up with my grandfather. I still have those stories and treasure them. In his trust, he included a line for each of us and left each grandchild some money. That part was also great! But the money is long gone. The stories he gave us are still with me today, and I want to be sure my clients are inspired to share their values and stories in much the same way.

How confident are you that you have Peril #9 solved?

<u>Circle One Number:</u>

(Not solved) 1 2 3 4 5 6 7 8 9 10 (Perfectly solved!)

Peril #10

The next Peril is a simple one to learn and likely a more challenging one to complete: Peril #10 is failing to organize and consolidate your financial affairs.

Have you ever opened a bank account because they were giving away free toasters or a free deposit? We may not be in a hurry to admit it, but it happens. Many of us have a variety of different bank accounts, all at different banks, and all based at different branches. Your investments are likely divided among different advisors, too. Even someone helping to manage the simplest estate will meet enormous added cost and complexity after you pass away if your money and investments are spread out.

When we work with you at Keystone Law Firm, we help you during our process to make sure you find and identify everything. We ask questions to help spark your memory and discover everything. Why do you have all these different accounts? Can we consolidate things? Do we know where everything is? We will then help you identify a central spot where everything can be listed.

How confident are you that you have Peril #10 solved?

<u>Circle One Number:</u>

(Not solved) 1   2   3   4   5   6   7   8   9   10 (Perfectly solved!)

Peril #11

Peril #11 is failing to pass along passwords, usernames, and online accounts. It was not so long ago that the most important items to keep secure were your safe deposit box key, your bankbooks, and your investment folders. Today, maintaining a safe and secure place where you house your electronic "keys" or passwords is equally important. Failing to secure these in one place and make sure someone knows how to locate them can wind up causing those online accounts to be frozen should you become incapacitated or pass away.

Did you know that online accounts can be frozen the moment the institution learns you are either incapacitated or have passed away? There's likely no way to access any of these—user names and passwords—without getting a court order. Yahoo, Gmail, Capital One, and other online companies have very specific "terms of service" that you agreed to when you signed up for their service. In almost every instance, the terms of service state that your account may be frozen once they learn of your incapacity or death.

When you prepare your estate and update it throughout your life, collect your passwords, email accounts, and user names. It is nearly impossible to NOT leave behind some type of digital footprint. The more information you can provide for those helping to administer your estate, the easier it will be to take care of you.

How confident are you that you have Peril #11 solved?

Circle One Number:

(Not solved) 1 2 3 4 5 6 7 8 9 10 (Perfectly solved!)

Peril #12

Peril #12 is failing to keep your plan current every day.

Think of a time when you stepped up to pay for something with a credit card and immediately learned the card expired? Perhaps you missed the new card in the mail or simply forgot to activate it. It doesn't matter, because the expired card won't buy you even a stick of gum. It's easy to forget to update things. Similarly, even the best-drafted estate plan becomes less relevant over time.

How frequently must you update your estate plan? The truth is no one answer is correct for every person. The best answer is that your estate plan must be perfect the day you die or become incapacitated. If your plan is not perfect, there will likely be unnecessary fees, taxes, costs, and delays waiting just around the corner.

Traditional estate planning works like this: You arrive for a consultation and the attorney charges $3,000-$6,000 for what is known as comprehensive estate planning. This process is different than when you go to a general practice lawyer who pulls a form out, has her secretary fill in the blanks, you sign it, and she collects your check. Comprehensive estate planning goes through many dimensions of getting your affairs in order and gets you fully squared away.

So the attorney then says, "Congratulations! You are now up to date!"

It's a good day.

Have you done a will or trust in the past? And are you 100% confident that your plan will be implemented exactly as you want, paying as little as legally possible in fees, court costs, and taxes if something happened to you right now? When I ask this question in group settings, about half of the group will say they have done a will or trust before. Yet, when I ask how many of those people are 100% confident with their estate plan, all but one or two hands drop. Often, those hands still in the air are already my clients.

Here's the problem. Most traditional estate planning firms ignore the most important fact: you aren't planning to die the day you sign your documents. Most of these firms have no mechanism to keep clients' estate plans current. The reality is estate plans are drafted around all kinds of different laws. In the state of Arizona, there are three major sections of law we must deal with: trust, tax, and probate laws. What's more is we must contend with all the Arizona court opinions interpreting these laws as it pertains to certain specific facts. This set of laws is overlaid on top of another whole set of laws at the federal level, which are also interpreted by federal case decisions.

Monitoring these detailed laws and how they mesh with one another and fit among different variables of each specific situation is critical. This is MY job. It's what I do. You should not have to worry about these changes and laws—your attorney should take that responsibility off your plate.

Some avoid planning their estates because they believe the plan is set in stone and hard to change. Your estate plan, once finished, is not and should not be set in stone.

It should be easy for you to make changes anytime you want. We encourage our clients to make changes as often as they need it. There are a few very rarely used estate-planning techniques that actually are set in stone, but that is not the norm.

No one wants outdated documents in their estate plan. Let's revisit the case I mentioned before regarding my client whose husband is in the conservatorship case. Despite the fact that she had a trust and a power of attorney, the age of these documents concerned their financial institution's compliance department. The financial institution rejected them to protect themselves. After years and dollars spent and many court dates, the financial institution WAS protected. The cost of that protection was my client's dollars—thousands of dollars—my client's time and privacy, and the time and privacy of her husband.

Please don't let this happen to you.

Arizona does not have a law that requires a third party like a bank or financial institution to honor your power of attorney. This is a weakness in Arizona's legal system. Because of this, financial institutions can and often do reject a valid power of attorney.

If you could see an example of a court docket for a conservator case, you would see hundreds of lines with each one representing billable hours. The probate court rules require that attorneys' bill hourly for this work. There's just no way to bill flat fees as an attorney on these cases.

The result is an incredibly expensive bill for anything filed because it must be drafted by one attorney and then read by the other attorney, and then he or she then must generate a response. Then, I must read the response, draft a reply, and so on, and so on.

Having an estate planning attorney that you can trust to keep your plans up-to-date is priceless—in dollars and in peace of mind.

How confident are you that you have Peril #12 solved?

Circle One Number:

(Not solved) 1 2 3 4 5 6 7 8 9 10 (Perfectly solved!)

How Confident Are You with Your Situation?

Record and add up your scores here:

Peril #1_____

Peril #2_____

Peril #3_____

Peril #4 _____

Peril #5_____

Peril #6_____

Peril #7_____

Peril #8_____

Peril #9_____

Peril #10_____

Peril #11_____

Peril #12_____

_____**Your Total Confidence Score**

What your score means:

If you have less than 108—A score below 108 means you *COULD* end up paying too much for probate, taxes and attorneys' fees.

If you have greater than 108 but less than 115—A score of above 108 but still below 115 means you may or may not be well-prepared. We recommend a review.

If you have greater than 115—We like our clients to score ABOVE 115 to be sure their estate plans are fully prepared and ready when they are needed.

Why use Keystone Law Firm?

There are two compelling reasons to work with Keystone Law Firm.

I have created a process for our estate planning clients that is affordable and ongoing. When a client engages us, our priority is to protect them and their estate from unnecessary probate, attorney fees, and taxes. It is my personal mission to be sure our clients always maintain updated plans. Our solution to this is our **TrustCare™** program. This program is not a document, and it's not a trust. Having learned early on that many people have had a document, a trust, or something else prepared, and they still ended up in probate, I knew I wanted to develop a system that would provide lifetime protection. Our **TrustCare™** program provides for a lifetime relationship with Keystone Law Firm and our team. This means your entire plan is protected for life. As a member, you can avoid all 12 of the Perils outlined here.

Imagine: as a **TrustCare™**, you have lifetime access to your estate planning attorney to answer any questions at any time—without any hourly bills. As a member of this program, you may completely avoid probate court during your lifetime and after your death. With our oversight, you have the confidence and peace of mind in knowing all of your affairs are consistently maintained and are completely private among you and those you designate to have authority. We are with you throughout your life, and we are also there when you or your spouse passes away.

Because of our careful oversight, we work hard to make winding up your affairs as easy as possible. We work with your handpicked fiduciary to distribute your affairs exactly as you have arranged them.

Estate planning is complicated. So is heart surgery. Yet people don't avoid heart surgery when they need it. I meet people every day that explain they are overwhelmed by the complexity of estate planning—so much so that they procrastinate in taking the necessary steps.

If this is you, I can help explain all components of the process and how everything works in a very clear and understandable process. What's most important is that you truly understand what not having a plan means for you. The results may not be as serious as delaying heart surgery, but they could be as heartbreaking.

You not only have our word, you have a written guarantee!

Each time I take on a new estate-planning client, I present each of these promises in writing as part of the **TrustCare**™ program. And, if something ends up going through probate, I PAY THE FEES. It is my job to keep probate far away from you and your affairs. I take my job very seriously.

The cornerstone of this guarantee is your living trust. We absolutely rely on a living trust as the backbone of this plan and we make sure it will NOT become outdated because of any changing laws, because your desires have changed, or because you simply don't like that plan anymore.

Think back to your life just 5 years ago. Where were you living? What occupied your thoughts? Which children did you like? A living trust is called "living" precisely because as you live, you are expected to change things in your life. Our basic trust packages include at least 17 different documents that we use to get everyone up to speed and keep them there.

Whether you have a trust already or are starting from scratch, this is the foundation of the plan that avoids probate, avoids guardianship, and avoids conservatorship.

It is important to mention that not everyone needs to be our client; and we are not for everyone. As the owner and managing attorney at Keystone Law Firm, I am very selective about who we bring into our lives. We care about our clients and we want to enjoy our work. To help us be sure this balance is maintained, we have rules governing who should be a **TrustCare™** and our first rule is: we will only accept nice people who want our help. In fact, we have a strict "No curmudgeons policy". This protects our wonderful current clients and it makes any curmudgeons free to find a law firm that matches their personality!

In addition to our first rule, there are other criteria that our prospective clients must meet to assure they will benefit from our **TrustCare™** program. Answering yes to ANY of these qualifies you (providing you are NOT a curmudgeon).

- **Do you have real estate with equity valued at more than $75,000?**
- **Do you own more than one piece of property?**
- **Do you have property in more than one state?**
- **Do you have more than $50,000 of anything else?**
- **Do you have a life-partner situation?**
- **Do you have children under 18?**
- **Do you plan to disinherit anyone?**
- **Do you plan to do *anything other* than equally distribute your assets to your children?**
- **Do you want to protect inheritances you leave behind from being lost to bankruptcy, creditors, lawsuits, or children's divorces?**

Once again, our **TrustCare**™ members are guaranteed to avoid probate. Our process is structured so that we walk side-by-side with our clients every step of the way to make sure that everything is protected. Then, after everything is protected, you have the full benefit of lifetime updates, advice, and handholding with your family through the entire process.

How much does this cost?

No one wants to fall prey to any of the 12 Perils of Estate Planning. Here is the question most people want the answer to right away: *how much does it cost?*

> ***You probably want to compromise elsewhere, and invest in the best lawyer.***

There are three costs to consider if you are price shopping: setting up the legal documents, funding your trust, and keeping everything up-to-date over time.

The first component, your legal documents, is where we prepare a plan putting all of the 18 necessary documents in place, written exactly how you want.

Next, all of your assets are funded to your trust. Here's an example of what happens if you don't fund your trust. Let's say I draft a trust directing everything be left to your spouse. Then, you get a life insurance policy naming Susie Shmoozy as your beneficiary. Who do you think gets the life insurance policy? It's Susie Shmoozy. We make sure your plan will play out exactly as you intend it by giving you specific funding instructions for each account, insurance, property, etc.

Finally, all that remains is our careful oversight through our **TrustCare™** Membership plan to keep everything up-to-date so that the day you are incapacitated or the day you pass away, your plan is ready.

Our pricing structure is transparent. We charge flat fees for all of our estate planning services. Because there are many different people with many different needs, I have developed a structure for many different levels of services covering the three different costs outlined above.

To set up the legal documents, our Starter Trust estate-planning package (under two thousand dollars) permits us to offer an affordable option for a simple plan. We also have trust packages that offer additional protections and tools that go beyond the Starter Trust for other needs.

With the funding of your trust, most of our clients do their own funding, with our firm handling only the real estate and business transactions. When it comes to all of your other financial and insurance assets, we create a specific checklist for you, advising you of exactly what to do with each one.

To keep your plan up-to-date, our on-going services in the **TrustCare™** program is another flat fee too. The annual fee is about what I charge for ONE HOUR of my time per year. This allows me to give my estate planning clients a full YEAR of services AND the probate guarantee. This means any changes you must make to your documents annually or any help you need in updating items if the law changes, is FULLY included in this one low, annual fee. When you call with a question or you are confused by something weird you received in the mail—we are here for you and there are no extra hourly charges.

If you are afraid of the cost, ask yourself this question: What is the cost of getting a good plan compared to the cost of not doing a plan at all. There is a cost with either decision.

Consider this. The cost of a sound estate plan is composed of three parts:

1. The cost of setting up all of the initial legal documents
2. The cost of making sure all of your assets (Bank accounts, financial investments, insurance policies, real estate, and business entities) are coordinated and directed to your legal documents.
3. The cost of ongoing updates as your life changes or as the law changes (the last thing you want is to put all of your effort, time and money into creating a great plan just to watch it become less and less relevant over time because updates are not made).

The cost of not having an estate plan also breaks down into parts—two parts:

1. **The lifetime cost**
2. **The after-death cost**

When you do not have the right documents in place throughout your life, you are open to the risk of having to be controlled by the court guardianship or conservatorship process. When people become incapacitated, these lawsuits spring up as officials and your family attempt to take care of you. Costs to initially set up a conservatorship are between $5,000 and $10,000. This isn't the end of it; the cost continues annually. There are even more costs after the person dies as tax consequences arise.

While it is difficult to estimate anyone's tax bill because it can vary drastically from one person to the next, the current estate tax rate is as high as 40 percent. When someone passes away, I estimate the tax bill for a very simple estate without any planning to be approximately $5,000. Naturally, when numerous bank accounts, investment accounts, and real estate are involved and improperly structured, the taxes can increase exponentially.

Summarizing all of these what-if situations can be tricky, yet the bottom line is that deciding not to have a plan can cost a minimum of $20,000. And that's for a "simple" estate.

What is not figured in here are the lost time and the increased misery of having to manage probate. Imagine years of public court proceedings while you are alive and one to two years of probate proceedings after you die. How much is avoiding this worth to you or your family?

It makes perfect sense to invest now while the costs are manageable and the decisions will be to your satisfaction.

My Irresistible Offer

By now you have heard that my work is my passion. I want EVERYBODY to have the very best possible opportunity to get his or her affairs in order—I don't want price to be the barrier! That's why I have created a special offer—specifically for those who have requested my book.

Give me ONE hour of your time

I invite you to visit my office, sit down with my staff, and share your story. I will be able to go through all of your information and provide you with my best recommendations for your estate plan.

Here's how it works:

1. **YOU call our office today and say, "I'm ready to create my estate plan".**

2. **Our office will set you up with an appointment that works for your schedule.**

3. **YOU prepare to talk about your situation and come to your appointment.**

4. **We will go over your situation, listen to your goals, and share our suggestions for a airtight plan for you.**

5. **You will see how simple I have made the process, and we will get started preparing your plan.**

I look forward to helping you achieve the very best results.

Francisco P. Swint

Pack Your Parachute

Keeping Peril Out of Your Estate Plan!

Learn MORE about how WE can create an IRON-CLAD estate plan for you

Call our office TODAY!

480-418-1776

Make your appointment for your

FREE ASSESSMENT

Feel secure.
Protect Your Assets.

We'll create your guaranteed estate plan!

My last words: Francisco P. Sirvent

If you read my book you learned how it is possible for the best intentions to go awry and how preparation can lock down your definitive choices in your favor. Hopefully, you also learned how important it is to me to truly preserve the valuable assets my clients have worked so hard to save and collect.

As you know I chose this practice of law because I really want to help people—I sleep better at night knowing my clients' assets are safeguarded and their plans, secure.

It is my hope that this book gave you value and insight into how YOU hold the key to making sound decisions and taking actions that will protect and give value for many, many years.

You won't lose a single thing in meeting with me because the first consultation is absolutely free.

Just send an email to info@keystonelawfirm.com or call 480-209-6942.

I am truly hopeful that I was able to bring some clarity to the notion of preparing your estate plan.

Warmest Regards,

Francisco P. Sirvent

If you haven't read Francisco's second book...

Your Arizona Probate Guidebook

Help for Arizonans in Probate: A Hand When It's Needed Most

Read this excerpt here to begin to learn how Arizona probate works and what can go wrong when it is not approached correctly.

Introduction to Probate

Probate is the process of transferring money or property <u>from</u> the name of a deceased person <u>to</u> the name of the rightful heirs. The local Superior Court probate division oversees the process.

You must go through probate if any of these things happen:

1. A bank, title company, lawyer, investment institution, insurance company, says you need:
   a. "Letters of Appointment"
   b. "Letters of Administration"
   c. "Letters of Executor"
   d. "Appointment as Personal Representative", or
   e. Anything similar to any of the above.
2. You want absolute certainty that all of the decedent's creditors are cut off from chasing after your inheritance.

> **Problem Spotter:**
>
> Lack of transparency is a very common complaint. Even if you are the authorized PR, you have a duty to be transparent.

3. Family members disagree about who should get what from the estate or who should be in charge of administering the estate.
4. While someone is still living, if they either did not have powers of attorney, or if others are not honoring their powers of attorney, or they are threatening to do themselves harm. (This is a reference to probate cases that occur during life: conservatorships & guardianships. This book is not going to discuss those issues. If you want to know more about them, contact our office.

There are three basic steps of probate administration: (1) collect, protect and manage the assets, (2) pay claims, taxes and costs of administration, and then (3) distribute estate assets.

Probate takes a long time

The fastest probate cases take *at least* six months. There is no getting around that. If there are any problems or delays along the way, an "easy" probate can take twelve months and a complicated probate case can take many years! So be prepared to tell everyone else involved that this is slow by design.

Difference Levels of Probate

Arizona has five different levels of probate that increase in complexity.
1. Transfer by Small Estate Affidavit,
2. Summary Administration,
3. Informal Probate,
4. Formal Probate, and
5. Supervised Administration

Levels 1 through 3 are suitable when the money and property values are small, there is no challenge, and either an original Will exists or the family members all agree about who should be the court-appointed personal representative. Levels 4 and 5 provide additional layers of protection to the people involved in the probate case when necessary.

Levels 4 and 5 should only be attempted with the help of an attorney.

Contact Keystone Law Firm to request your free copy of

Your Arizona Probate Guidebook

Help for Arizonans in Probate: A Hand When It's Needed Most

Call us today at

480-418-1776

Notes:

Notes:

Made in the USA
Middletown, DE
12 May 2024

54132928R00040